DO YOU WANT A PET TARANTULA?

THAT'S AN ODD PET!

BY LOUIS MALLORY

Enslow PUBLISHING

Please visit our website, www.enslow.com. For a free color catalog of all our high-quality books, call toll free 1-800-398-2504 or fax 1-877-980-4454.

Cataloging-in-Publication Data

Names: Mallory, Louis.
Title: Do you want a pet tarantula? / Louis Mallory.
Description: Buffalo, NY : Enslow Publishing, 2025. | Series: That's an odd pet! | Includes glossary and index.
Identifiers: ISBN 9781978540866 (pbk.) | ISBN 9781978540873 (library bound) | ISBN 9781978540880 (ebook)
Subjects: LCSH: Tarantulas as pets–Juvenile literature.
Classification: LCC SF459.T37 M35 2025 | DDC 639'.7–dc23

Published in 2025 by
Enslow Publishing
2544 Clinton Street
Buffalo, NY 14224

Portions of this work were originally authored by Patrick Hely and published as *Tarantulas*. All new material in this edition is authored by Louis Mallory.

Designer: Claire Zimmermann
Editor: Natalie Humphrey

Photo credits: Cover (photo) Ernie Cooper/Shutterstock.com; Series Art (title and heading font, texture) Gleb Guralnyk/Shutterstock.com; Series Art (background retro swirl) ChekmanDaria/Shutterstock.com; Series Art (corner dots) Romanova Ekaterina/Shutterstock.com; Series Art (body text boxes, page number background shape) Angie Makes/Shutterstock.com; Series Art (hand-drawn doodles) yugoro/Shutterstock.com; p. 5 Leena Robinson/Shutterstock.com; p. 7 iLight photo/Shutterstock.com; p. 9 monster_code/Shutterstock.com; p. 11 Vladimira Pufflerova/Shutterstock.com; p. 13 SmirMaxStock/Shutterstock.com; p. 15 Close to Me Photography/Shutterstock.com; p. 17 Cornel Constantin/Shutterstock.com; p. 19 Gayleen Froese/Shutterstock.com.

Printed in the United States of America

CPSIA compliance information: Batch #CSENS25: For further information contact Enslow Publishing at 1-800-398-2504.

CONTENTS

Words in the glossary appear in **bold** type the first time they are used in the text.

ODD SPIDERS

For most people, a spider in their house is their worst nightmare. But some people think the biggest spiders in the world, tarantulas, make the best pets! Pet tarantulas might look scary, but there are a lot of great things about owning a pet spider.

JUST THE FACTS!

The Goliath bird-eating spider is the largest **arachnid** in the world. It is a kind of tarantula! It is unlikely you would keep this kind of spider as a pet.

While tarantulas are usually quiet, some tarantulas can hiss when they sense danger.

If you're looking for a pet that's easier to care for, a tarantula might be the perfect pet for you. Many tarantulas are **docile** and spend most of their time hiding.

HUGE TARANTULAS

Tarantulas are huge! Tarantulas can be as big as your hand, but some can be bigger. Their eight legs are long and thin. Each leg has tiny claws and hairs that help them climb. They also have large **fangs** to help them catch and hold **prey**.

Tarantulas sense the world with their bodies. Tarantulas are covered with hairs that feel tiny **vibrations** in the ground. This is how they know if something is moving nearby.

Tarantulas have eight eyes, but they can't see very well.

JUST THE FACTS!

Tarantulas don't have noses, but they can still sense smells! They have special hairs on the ends of their legs that are used to "smell" prey or other spiders.

A WARM HOME

Most tarantulas live in South and Central America, but some live in Africa, Southeast Asia, the Southwestern United States, and Australia.

Like most spiders, tarantulas make silk in their bodies. However, tarantulas don't usually spin webs to catch prey.

JUST THE FACTS!

Tarantulas are usually active at night and during the early morning. They hunt by hiding and surprising prey that wanders by.

Tarantulas love eating bugs, but larger tarantulas may also eat frogs, toads, birds, and small **rodents**.

Instead, most tarantulas use their silk to line their **burrows**. This makes it harder for other bugs and predators to enter their home. Tarantulas also use their silk on their feet to help them stick to smooth surfaces.

SO MANY SPIDERS

There are hundreds of different species, or kinds, of tarantulas found in the wild. Scientists believe there could be around 1,000 different species of tarantulas. With so many different kinds, how do you pick your perfect pet?

JUST THE FACTS!

One of the most common types of pet tarantulas is the Mexican red-knee tarantula.

Mexican red-knee tarantulas are gentle, making them great pets, but they can cost a lot of money to own!

Not every tarantula would make a good pet. Some are more active. Some barely move at all. Many tarantulas are expensive, or cost a lot of money. Some tarantulas can only be found in the wild and should never be kept as pets.

SPIDER TANKS

Before you bring a tarantula home, make sure you have a **tank** for it. Tarantulas have different needs based on how they live in the wild. Some tarantulas live in trees. They like a tall tank with branches to climb. Others live close to the ground and need more bedding.

All tanks need a few inches of bedding for your spider to dig in. Your tank also needs to have a good lid that locks.

Tarantula tanks should be kept in a warm room so your spider doesn't get too cold.

JUST THE FACTS!

Tarantulas that make burrows need special tanks that are wider than they are tall. This is so that they don't fall and hurt themselves!

TARANTULA FOOD

Tarantulas might be big spiders, but it isn't too hard to keep them fed. Tarantulas mostly eat small bugs. Crickets are a common choice for tarantulas! You can buy feeder crickets at a pet store. Most tarantulas eat only about two crickets a week but can eat more. Tarantulas are usually hungrier after molting.

JUST THE FACTS!

Tarantulas usually leave leftover food and poop in certain areas of their tank. You may need to spot clean these areas to keep your tarantula's tank clean.

If your tarantula doesn't eat all the crickets you give it, make sure to take out any living crickets it leaves behind so the crickets don't hurt your pet!

It's important to feed your crickets well before they're fed to a tarantula. This is called "gut-loading" your crickets.

MOLTING

Tarantulas molt as they grow. Never bother a tarantula when it's molting. Molting tarantulas often lie on their backs and may look dead. After molting, the spider's body is soft and tender. It may take a few days for your tarantula's new **exoskeleton** to harden.

Tarantulas can have what is called a "bad molt" that results in cuts or lost legs. Don't worry, though, your tarantula may be able to regrow its lost leg!

Young tarantulas will molt more often than older tarantulas.

JUST THE FACTS!

Tarantulas do not usually need to visit a vet. But, if you are worried your tarantula might be sick, finding a vet that takes care of bugs is important.

WATCH OUT!

While it doesn't happen often, tarantulas can bite! A tarantula that's treated properly and regularly handled won't usually bite. But when it does, it usually feels like a bee sting. Bites don't usually cause issues unless you're **allergic** to tarantula bites.

JUST THE FACTS!

If you're worried about spider bites or thrown hairs, you can protect yourself! Wearing gloves and safety goggles can keep your hands and eyes safe.

While tarantula fangs can be big, their mouths aren't usually strong enough to break human skin.

Some kinds of tarantulas can "throw" hairs from their body when they sense trouble. These hairs may stick to the eyes and nose of predators. They can be itchy or painful for people.

HANDLING TARANTULAS

Tarantulas shouldn't be handled too often. If you want to pick up your tarantula, you can use a pair of **forceps** with soft tips. Gently hold your tarantula between its second and third set of legs. You can also use a large, clear cup to catch your spider. Never squeeze your tarantula.

Some spiders can live for a long time. Female tarantulas usually live longer than males. A female that has been well cared for may live for 30 years!

TAKING CARE OF YOUR TARANTULA!

Make sure your tarantula's tank is right for the type of tarantula it is.

Feed your tarantula crickets regularly and moths, cockroaches, and other small bugs as treats.

Give your tarantula a shallow bowl with fresh water.

Keep the lid on your tarantula's tank when you're not handling it.

Make sure your tarantula's tank has plenty of bedding for it to dig in.

Keep in mind that male tarantulas usually live for around 10 years while females can live up to 30 years.

JUST THE FACTS!

In some places, like New York City, it's illegal to keep tarantulas as pets. Make sure to check your local laws before buying a tarantula.

GLOSSARY

allergic: A body's sensitivity to usually harmless things in the surroundings, such as dust, pollen, or mold.

arachnid: One of a large class of small animals that includes spiders, scorpions, ticks, daddy longlegs, and mites.

burrow: A hole in the ground an animal uses to live or hide in.

docile: Easy to handle or control.

exoskeleton: The hard outer covering of an animal's body.

fang: A long, pointed tooth.

forceps: A tool used to pick up and hold something.

prey: An animal that is hunted by other animals for food.

rodent: A small, furry animal with large front teeth, such as a mouse or rat.

tank: A large container made for some pets to live in.

vibration: A rapid movement back and forth.

FOR MORE INFORMATION

Books

Becker, Trudy. *Tarantulas*. Lake Elmo, MN: Focus Readers, 2023.

Jaycox, Jaclyn. *Tarantulas*. Oxford, England: Raintree, 2021.

Websites

Britannica Kids: Tarantula
https://kids.britannica.com/kids/article/tarantula/353837
Learn more facts about tarantulas.

National Geographic Kids: Tarantula
www.kids.nationalgeographic.com/animals/invertebrates/facts/tarantula
Learn more about how tarantulas live in the wild.

Publisher's note to educators and parents: Our editors have carefully reviewed these websites to ensure that they are suitable for students. Many websites change frequently, however, and we cannot guarantee that a site's future contents will continue to meet our high standards of quality and educational value. Be advised that students should be closely supervised whenever they access the internet.

INDEX